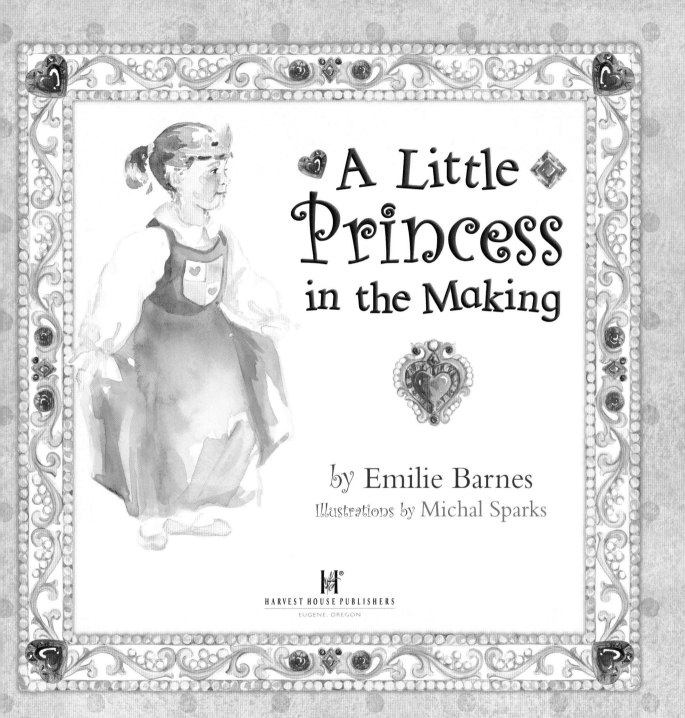

A Little Princess in the Making

by Emilie Barnes

Illustrations by Michal Sparks

HARVEST HOUSE PUBLISHERS
EUGENE, OREGON

A Little Princess in the Making

Copyright © 2007 Emilie Barnes and Anne Christian Buchanan
Published by Harvest House Publishers
Eugene, OR 97402
ISBN-13: 978-0-7369-1855-8
ISBN-10: 0-7369-1855-8

All works of art reproduced in this book are copyrighted by Michal Sparks and may
not be reproduced without the artist's permission. For more information regarding art
featured in this book, please contact:

Mr. Gifford B. Bowne II
Indigo Gate
1 Pegasus Drive
Colts Neck, NJ 07722
(732) 577-9333

Design and Production: Garborg Design Works, Minneapolis, Minnesota

Printed in China

08 09 10 11 / LP / 5 4

Contents

I'm a Little Princess!

Welcome to the castle! I'm Princess Emilie Marie, and I'm happy that you're learning how to be a little princess with me! Someday we'll both be queens with beautiful gowns and sparkly crowns, but right now we're princesses in training. We're learning what to do and what to say so that we can be loving and kind ladies.

I love to pick bouquets from the garden and dress up fancy for balls and set the table for play tea parties, don't you? I also love learning how to set the table for real and knowing how to act at real parties. I'm learning good *manners*—things I do which show that I'm a princess, both inside and out!

Would you like to start your princess training with me? I'm glad you would! Let's hold hands, and we can do this together!

I'm a Little Princess when I...

❥ Care for My Castle ❥

My castle is beautiful! And yours is very special, too! In my castle I have balls and plays and performances every day with my favorite dress-up clothes and dolls and tea party dishes. In fact, my castle—which is where I live, of course—is the very best place to begin my princess training. The people who love me live there, and it's where I feel safe and happy.

When I'm at home in my castle, I have lots of chances to use the magic kingdom words. I say these words when I need something or when someone does something nice for me or when I do something wrong. (Even princesses goof up sometimes!) And these magic words always work!

You're Welcome

They make me feel happy, and they make everyone around me feel happy, too. Are you ready to learn them? Here they are—

Please.
Thank you.
Excuse me.
I'm sorry.

When you're at home with your family, you can practice acting like a princess. You can be kind. You can be helpful. You can be giving. You can be obedient.

And did you know that every princess has a special rule she follows? It even has a royal-sounding name! It's called the Golden Rule:

Do unto others as you would have them do unto you.

This just means that you can treat people in the way that *you* would like to be treated. Do you like to get help making your bed or picking up your toys? Sure! Then you can *help* others. Do you like getting gifts? Of course! Then you can *give* to others. Do you like for things to be fair? Yes! Then you can *play fair* with others.

When you're at home in your castle, you can start your princess training by listening to the king and queen (those are your parents) and doing what they ask. Put your wands and crowns away. Come when you're called. Always tell the truth. Be kind to your brothers and sisters and pets.

What a great start! Every little princess cares for her castle, and you're doing a fantastic job!

I'm a Little Princess when I...

❧ Am a Good Friend ❧

I just love tea parties, don't you? Inviting friends (even if they are all dolls!), dressing up, picking flowers for the tea table, serving real or pretend treats…. I can show good friendship manners—and show that I'm a real princess—by being a proper party host. And the best way I can do this is by *sharing* with others.

A true princess always shares with others—she shares her ideas, her dolls, and her creativity. She knows that waiting patiently and taking turns make her pretty both inside and out.

You can also be a princess by being honest and truthful. When you're playing with other little princes and princesses, be fair and keep your promises. It's fine to have secrets between friends—as long as they are nice ones and nobody feels left out. The main thing is to include everybody. *Everyone* plays!

It's easy to be a good friend when you think about how the other person feels. Do you like it when others listen to you? Then listen to them! Do you feel good when someone lets you go first or gives you the prettiest cupcake? You can do the same for them!

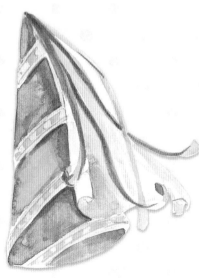

The heart of playtime manners is to be a good friend. And you're always a princess when you use your best friendship manners!

I'm a Little Princess when I...

🌑 Travel Through My Kingdom 🌑

Step right up into my horse-drawn carriage! We're going to drive away from the castle and travel through our beautiful kingdom. There's so much to do and see—lovely gardens to visit (with swingsets!), kind and gentle people to play with (grandparents!), and other kind princes and princesses to get to know (new friends!).

Every good princess needs to know how to act when she's out in the world. And using your very best manners will show everyone what a polite little girl you are—a real princess in the making!

Sometimes when you're out traveling through your kingdom, you might meet someone who looks or acts a little different. Maybe the clothes the other person wears look different from yours, or the person is in a wheelchair, or they speak differently. But inside, they are just the same as you. They deserve a princess's friendship, too!

Princesses are always meeting new people! When you meet someone, smile at them and say "hello." You can shake their hand—that's a *very* ladylike thing to do. (It might even be fun to curtsy!) Right now, it's best to meet new people when you're with your parents or another adult that you know very well. That way, you can stay safe *and* learn what to do and say. When you're done, be sure to say a friendly "goodbye." It's also sweet to say, "It was very nice to meet you!"

Princesses always show kindness to others by calling them what they would like to be called—Miss Diamond or Mr. Emerald or Dr. Ruby. That shows kindness and respect. (Sometimes people even call *me* Princess Emilie Marie in return!)

Do you still remember the Golden Rule? I'm glad you do! If you remember to treat others as you would like to be treated, it's easy to know what to do and say when you're out in your kingdom!

4

I'm a Little Princess when I...

💿 Make Myself Pretty 💿

What a lovely pink dress you have on! And what a beautiful, sparkly silver tiara! And with your velvet cape and those glittery shoes—you really look the part of the perfect little princess!

I like to wear pretty clothes also, but a big part of my princess training is learning to care for myself. My crown looks so much better when my hair is combed and clean. My smile is brighter when I've brushed my teeth. (And I'm learning to floss them, too!) The queen is teaching me how to sort laundry (lights and darks!) so that I always have clean clothes to wear.

The king and queen (my parents) are teaching me how to make myself pretty on the outside with clean hair, teeth, and clothes. But they're also teaching me that it's important to be pretty on the *inside*. That's why I practice caring for myself every day. I try not to grumble or complain when I'm asked to help sort laundry or wash my face. If the queen (my mom) wants me to change my clothes, it's important that I obey her. She knows that I might tear my gown playing in the sandbox, or trip on my sparkly high heels skipping through the store!

When I'm sick, it's hard to pretend I'm a princess (even though I really am one!). Did you know that good manners can help keep you healthy? They can! I'm careful to wash my hands a lot—especially after going to the bathroom and before I eat. If I am sick, I always blow my nose into a tissue and cover my cough. That way I help other people stay healthy.

It's fun to use my best manners to take care of myself—and I feel pretty as a princess when I do!

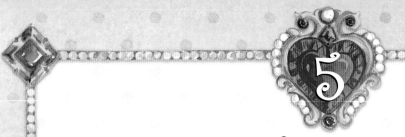

I'm a Little Princess when I...

❀ Dine at My Fancy Table ❀

Help! There's a dragon in the castle! *Gulp! Slurp! Snork!* Oh, wait…that's not a dragon. That's *me!* I guess I forgot to bring my princess manners to the table. I'm doing better, but every now and then I need to remind myself how a princess dines at her fancy table. Let's review this one together!

Princesses are strong and healthy girls. They ride horses, run fast through the castle grounds, and know how to scare off the occasional dragon. By eating healthy foods— fruits and vegetables, proteins, and vitamins—you can become a strong, healthy girl. Even if you don't think you will like something, be brave and give it a try! The dragon might not try broccoli or burritos, but you surely can. If something does taste terrible— or if you're allergic to it—a simple "No, thank you" will do.

A helpful princess always offers to help get the food ready (and sometimes she gets to use fun and safe kitchen tools!) or set the table— or even design some fancy place mats. When you're told it's time to eat, wash your hands and come to the table right away. Sit up straight

in your chair (that keeps your crown from falling off), keep your mouth closed when chewing your food, and say "Excuse me" or "I'm sorry" if you accidentally spill something or make a mistake.

Dragons always slink away from the table right when they finish their food, but a princess always asks, "May I please be excused?" before she waltzes off to play. Thank the cook for the tasty meal, and then you're on your way!

I'm a Little Princess when I...

Have a Grateful Heart

We've escaped the dragon, ridden in our horse-drawn carriage, and polished our tiaras. But before I go, let's talk about one final part to being a real princess—having a grateful heart.

Princesses come in all shapes, sizes, and colors. Some are short, some are tall. Some are blonde, some are brunette. Some are talkative, some are quiet. But all princesses have a heart filled with the jewels of kindness, love, and caring. In fact, two small words hold the key to a grateful heart. These are magic words:

Thank you.

These two simple words make everyone feel good—both the person being thanked *and* the person saying thank you! And even though you might not always be able to have tea in your fancy gown or dance in your sparkly shoes, you can *always* use these magic princess words. They always work, too!

Just about any time is a good time to use the magic "thank you" words. Whenever anyone says something nice to you, lends a helping hand, gives you a present, or invites you over for playtime or to a party, that's the right time to say "thank you."

You can say "thank you" in person, make a thank-you phone call, give a thank-you hug, or even draw a thank-you picture.

It's time for a curtsy and a good-bye hug.
You've done it! You're a real princess now!

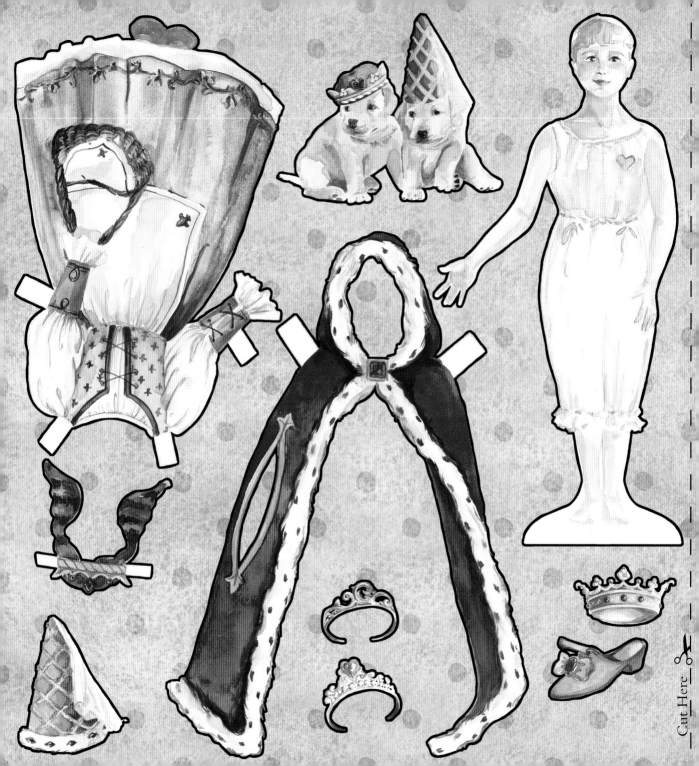

Cut Here